Forty percent of what we worry about
never happens. Thirty percent has already
happened. Twelve percent focused on opinions
or situations we cannot change. Ten percent on
our health, which only worsens it. Eight percent
concerns real problems we can influence.
Think: ninety-two percent of our worries are
needless!

Gass

Watch your thoughts,
they become your words
Watch your words,
they become your actions
Watch your actions,
they become your habits
Watch your habits,
they become your character
Watch your character,
it becomes your
destiny.

Anonymous

Life's up and downs provide windows of opportunity to determine your values and goals. Think of using all obstacles as stepping-stones to build the life you want.

Marsha Sinetar

Resentment is one burden that is incompatible with your success. Always be the first to forgive; and forgive yourself first always.

Dan Zadra

Always direct your thoughts to those truths that will give you confidence, hope, joy, love, thanksgiving and turn away your mind from those that inspire you with fear, sadness and depression.

Bertrand Wilberforce

Let go of your attachment to being right, and suddenly your mind is more open. You're able to benefit from the unique viewpoints of others, without being crippled by your own judgment.

Ralph Marston

Be yourself. Who else is better qualified?

Frank J. Giblin II

We get new ideas from God every hour of our day when we put our trust in Him -- but we have to follow that inspiration up with perspiration -- we have to work to prove our faith. Remember that the bee that hangs around the hive never gets any honey.

Albert E. Cliffe

. . .if we wait for the moment when everything, absolutely everything is ready, we shall never begin.

Ivan Turgenev

You don't have more problems than other people – you just think about them more often!

Gass

Because something is good doesn't mean it is
right for you.

Gass

One of the richest places on earth is the grave. So many of us die with unused talents.

Donovan Brown

Entrepreneurs are risk-takers, willing to roll the dice with their money or reputation on the line in support of an idea or enterprise. They willingly assume responsibility for the success or failure of a venture and are answerable for all it's facets. The buck not only stops at their desks, it starts there too.

Victor Kiam

Sometimes you have to move backward to get a step forward.

Amar Gopal Bose

Real difficulties can be overcome; it is only the imaginary ones that are unconquerable.

Theodore N. Vail

I have learned from experience that the greater part of our happiness or misery depends on our dispositions and not on our circumstances.

Martha Washington

We cannot direct the wind but we can adjust the sails.

Anonymous

What would you attempt to do if you knew you would not fail?

Robert Schuller

.

Act as if it were impossible to fail.

Dorothea Brand

When you make a mistake, don't look back at it long. Take the reason of the thing into your mind, and then look forward. Mistakes are lessons of wisdom. The past cannot be changed. The future is yet in your power.

Phyllis Bottome

Becoming a star may not be in your destiny, but being the best that you can be is a goal you can set for yourselves.

Bryan Lindsay

There is a transcendent power in example. We reform others unconsciously when we walk uprightly.

Anne Sophie Swetchine

Everything you want is out there waiting for you to ask. Everything you want also wants you. But you have to take action to get it.

Jack Canfield

Every trial, tribulation, question mark, perplexity, decision, burden, disappointment, heartache, calamity, tragedy, turmoil, loss, danger, exclusion, accusation, threat or act of the devil is within the scope of God's knowledge. He is sovereign; He has already worked it out. His ministering angels protect us. His precious blood covers us. His grace and mercy goes before us. Wow! What more do you need?

Thelma Wells

Recognise when something's dead. No amount of effort will resuscitate a corpse, so sign the death certificate, bury the past and get going. That doesn't mean you are quitting, it just means you are conserving your strength for things that count, for things you can do something about.

Gass

Don't let it get you down, how far you've got
to go. Look back and see how far you've
come.

Frank Murray

I can't do it never accomplished anything; I will try has performed wonders.

George P. Burnham

Attitude is a small thing that makes a big difference.

Anonymous

Hope becomes reality when people work together.

Anonymous

Never let yesterday use up today.

Rita M. Brown

Too often our actions are dictated not by a sense of purpose but by a need to please. We care so much about what certain people think, that with every step we look over our shoulders to see whether they are smiling or frowning . . . Living on purpose is the way to really live; anything else is just existing.

Gass

How can you be a victor if you run from conflict?

Donovan Brown

If you realise how powerful your thoughts are,
you would never think a negative thought.

Anonymous

We should watch the friends we keep for we become like the people we spend our time with. Life comes from the lips of the wise and death from the lips of fools.

Donovan Brown

Our friends should be companions who inspire
us, who help us rise to our best.

Joseph B. Wirthlin

We're products of our past but we don't have
to be prisoners of it!

Gass

Consider the rights of others before your own feelings, and the feelings of others before your own rights.

John Wooden

No matter how far you have gone on the wrong way turn back.

Turkish Proverb

There are two things to aim at in life; first get what you want and after that to enjoy it. Only the wisest of mankind achieve the second.

Legand Smith

We cannot do everything at once, but we can do something at once.

Calvin Coolidge

Excuses are the nails used to build a house of failure.

Don Wilder

Find a way, not an excuse.

Debbie Womelsduff

When one door of happiness closes, another opens; but often we look so long at the closed door that we do not see the one which has open for us.

Helen Keller

Positive communication, love and respect are the most important keys needed to build and continue a successful relation ship whatever the relationship.

Donovan Brown

A strong positive self-image is the best possible preparation for success.

Anonymous

Twenty years from now you'll be more disappointed by the things you didn't do, than by the ones you did. So throw off the bowlines. Sail away from your safe harbour. Catch the wind. Explore. Dream. Discover.

Mark Twain

Nothing happens until I make it happen.

Scott Wilson

Set your goal and focus on it.

Anonymous

Men are born to succeed, not fail.

Henry D. Thoreau

As simple as it sounds, we all must try to be the best person we can: by making the best choices, by making the most of the talents we've been given.

Mary Lou Retton

You won't find time for any thing. If you want time for something you have to make it.

Anonymous

You are the answer to some of your own prayers. Did you know that?

Donovan Brown

There is something good in all seeming failures.
You are not to see that now. Time will reveal
it. Be patient.

Sri Swami Sivananda

Things turn out best for the people who make the best out of the way things turn out.

Art Linkletter

When things are bad, we take comfort in the thought that they could always be worse. And when they are, we find hope in the thought that things are so bad that they have to get better.

Malcolm Forbes

Did you ever see an unhappy horse? Did you ever see bird that had the blues? One reason why birds and horses are not unhappy is because they are not trying to impress other birds and horses.

Dale Carnegie

Many people think that if they were only in some other place, or had some other job, they would be happy. Well, that is doubtful. So get as much happiness out of what you are doing as you can and don't put off being happy until some future date.

Dale Carnegie

Some men go through a forest and see
no firewood.

English Proverb

To forgive is to set a prisoner free and discover that prisoner was you.

Louis Smedes

There are three types of people in this world: those who make things happen, those who watch things happen and those who wonder what happened. We all have a choice. You can decide which type of person you want to be. I have always chosen to be in the first group.

Mary Kay Ash

Winners are the people who when the odds are stacked against them, and those around them have fallen, will have the courage to look within themselves and make the unbelievable believable, and the impossible possible.

C. Phillips

Why not learn to enjoy the little things there
are so many of them.

Anonymous

Change is important in life. Be willing to surrender what you are, for what you could become.

Anonymous

Courage is not the absence of fear, but rather the judgement that something else is more important than fear.

Anonymous

To avoid criticism do nothing, say nothing, be nothing.

Elbert Hubbard

Keep away from people who try to belittle your ambitions. Small people always do that, but the really great ones make you feel that you too, can become great.

Mark Twain

The bad stuff is easier to believe. Did you ever notice that?

Anonymous

Worrying is like being in a rocking chair; it gives you something to do but does not get you anywhere.

Anonymous

The only one thing I can change is myself, but sometimes that makes all of the difference.

Anonymous

You are your own raw material. When you know what you consist of and what you want to make of it, then you can invent yourself.

Orison S. Marden

What you do today can change the course of your life far into the future. Today is critical. Today really counts.

Ralph Mason, Jr

Opportunities multiply as they are seized; they die when neglected. Life is a long line of opportunities.

John Wicker

The country clubs, the cars the boats, your assets may be ample, but the best inheritance you can leave your kids is to be a good example.

Barry Spilchuk

We must become the change we want to see.

Mahatma Gandhi

A man can be as great as he wants to be. If
you believe in yourself and have the courage,
the determination, the dedication, the competitive
drive and if you are willing to sacrifice the little
things in life and pay the price for the things
that are worthwhile, it can be done.

Vince Lombardi

Go home and love your family.

Mother Teresa

Failure always results from saying yes to too many things. When you are spread too thin you become mediocre at everything and excellent at nothing.

Gass

One way to succeed is to make the maximum uses of the resources you have available to you. And not spend your time focusing on what others have available to them.

Donovan Brown

Do you want failure and unhappiness? Then try to please everyone.

Donovan Brown

I believe In God like I believe in the sun; not because I see It but because of It I see everything.

Anonymous

The men who try to do something and fail are Infinitely better than those who try to do nothing and succeed.

Lloyd Jones

How easily we give up.

Anonymous

You could be as successful or even more successful than the person or persons you admire. All you need to do Is get out of your comfort zone and take risks. No risk no reward.

Donovan Brown

A moment of thought before you act could save you a lifetime of regret. So think before you act.

Donovan Brown

Vision without action Is a daydream. Action without vision Is a nightmare. You have to take action as well as dream if you want to bring your vision into reality.

Donovan Brown

A journey of a thousand miles begins with a single step.

Japanese Proverb

A word of encouragement during a failure Is worth more than an hour of praise after success.

Anonymous

Do not let what you cannot do Interfere with
what you can do.

John Woode

... don't base God's love based on your circumstances; Instead look for Him In the midst of them.

Gass

Wise friends make you wise... you hurt yourself by going around with fools.

Gass

Determination gives you the resolve to keep going despite the roadblocks that lay the before you.

Denis Waitley

The fear of failure is often times the greatest
barrier to success.

Anonymous

If we did the things we are capable of we would astound ourselves.

Thomas Edison

Do It afraid.

Joyce Meyer

... you are Mine. When you pass through the waters, I will be with you; and when you pass through the rivers, they will not sweep over you. When you walk through the fire, you will not be burnt... For I am the Lord your God... you are precious and honoured In my sight and... I love you.

The Bible

Your greatest possession Is your next twenty-four hours. How will you spend It? Will you allow tv, pointless e-mails, unimportant tasks, telemarketers, the wrong crowd or other distractions to consume your day? If you do not decide how your day will be spent, count on It someone else will.

Gass

I'll give up tomorrow.

Anonymous

To get out of difficulty, one must usually go through It.

Anonymous

To do nothing Is within the power of us all.

Anonymous

Big jobs usually go to the men who prove their ability to outgrow small ones.

Ralph Emerson

If you worry about the future, and dwell on the past, you can't enjoy the present.

Emily Gibbons

Behind every successful man there are a lot of unsuccessful years.

Bob Brown

Aim at the sun and you may not reach it; but your arrow will fly far higher than if you had aimed at an object on a level with yourself.

Joel Hawes

Don't let life discourage you, everyone who got where he is had to begin where he was.

Richard Evans

Begin to weave and God will supply the thread.

German Proverb

If you change the way you think your life will follow. Have a defeated mentality and you will live a pitiful life. Have a positive mental attitude and your life will soar. So all you need to do is to change the way you think and your life will change with it, that is for better or for worst.

Donovan Brown

Had I not failed
I would have not succeeded.

Donovan Brown

Printed in the United Kingdom by
Lightning Source UK Ltd., Milton Keynes
137901UK00001B/74/P